CHRIS HODGES

WITH DUDLEY DELFFS

Out
of the
Cave

STUDY GUIDE | FIVE SESSIONS

HOW ELIJAH **EMBRACED GOD'S HOPE**
WHEN **DARKNESS** WAS ALL HE COULD SEE

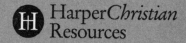

Harper*Christian*
Resources

Published in Nashville, Tennessee, by Harper*Christian* Resources, a registered trademark of HarperCollins Christian Publishing, Inc.

Published in association with Yates & Yates, www.yates2.com.

All Scripture quotations, unless otherwise indicated, are taken from The Holy Bible, New International Version®, NIV®. Copyright © 1973, 1978, 1984, 2011 by Biblica, Inc.™ Used by permission. All rights reserved worldwide.

Scripture quotations marked NLT are from the Holy Bible, New Living Translation. © 1996, 2004, 2007, 2013, 2015 by Tyndale House Foundation. Used by permission of Tyndale House Publishers, Inc., Carol Stream, Illinois 60188. All rights reserved.

Harper*Christian* Resources titles may be purchased in bulk for church, business, fundraising, or ministry use. For information, e-mail ResourceSpecialist@ChurchSource.com.

ISBN 978-0-310-11751-3 (softcover)
ISBN 978-0-310-11752-0 (ebook)

First Printing May 2021 / Printed in the United States of America

Contents

Introduction

No one is immune to depression—not Christians, not pastors, not even God's prophets. Perhaps there's no better case study for exploring the darkness of depression and the power of God's light than the life of the Old Testament prophet Elijah. Chosen by God to be his prophet to the people of Israel, Elijah nevertheless struggled to trust God's goodness and to experience his power in the midst of anxiety, fear, and uncertainty.

Elijah's experience reminds us that everyone is susceptible to depression. No matter how powerful, accomplished, or successful we may be, we can still succumb to fear, doubt, and a sense of hopelessness that robs us of our life's purpose and joy. Even when we're walking with God, as Elijah was, we can still stumble and get lost in the wilderness of tangled emotions.

But we don't have to stay there. Elijah's example reveals that God is always with us, even in the darkness of depression. Elijah's retreat into the cave of hopelessness and his life-changing encounter with God there reveal a path to our own way back into the light.

Most experts agree that depression is now the number one health problem in the world. Whether the into it descent is gradual or sudden, the impact of depression affects every area of a person's life. Compounding the problem, many people still stigmatize those who suffer from depression and other forms of mental illness. They sympathize when someone gets physically ill or suffers a bodily injury, yet they often dismiss the issues a person may have related to emotional and psychological health. Somehow, they assume, a person's emotional and mental health should be completely within his or her control at all times.

For followers of Jesus, this stigma is even greater. Many believers assume that God's peace, power, and protection should prevent them from feeling anxious, depressed, and afraid. But that's not what we find in the Bible. In fact, just the opposite! In God's Word, we're told to "fear not" at least 365 times—one for each day of the year—along with reminders of God's presence in the midst of any and every human emotion . . . including depression and anxiety.

Elijah's battle with depression and his God-inspired victory over it offer hope and healing for us today. Depression is a powerful and complex condition . . . but it can be overcome. In addition to seeking medical treatment, exploring talk therapy, and relying on God's Word within a trusted community of believers, we can also make changes in our lifestyle, attitude, and habits that facilitate the peace and joy we can experience in Christ.

We can follow Elijah's journey into the light of God's healing presence.

How to Use This Guide

Group Size

The *Out of the Cave* video study is designed to be experienced in a group setting (such as a Bible study, Sunday school class, or other small-group gathering) and also as an individual study. If you are doing the study as a group and the gathering is large, your leader may split everyone into smaller groups of five or six people to make sure everyone has enough time to participate in discussions.

Materials Needed

Everyone in your group will need a copy of this study guide, which includes the opening questions you will discuss, notes for video segments, directions for activities and discussion questions, and personal studies for between sessions. You may also want a copy of the book *Out of the Cave*, which provides further insights into the material you are covering in this study. To aid your study experience, you will be encouraged to read specific chapters in the book to prepare for the group's next meeting.

Facilitation

If you are doing the study with a group, you will need to appoint a person to serve as a facilitator. This person will be responsible for starting the video and keeping track of time during discussions and activities. (Note that the videos can be accessed at any time via the streaming code found on the inside front cover of this guide). Facilitators may also read questions aloud and monitor discussions, prompting participants to respond and assuring that everyone has the opportunity to participate. If you have been chosen for this role, there are additional resources in the back of this guide to help you lead your group through the study.

Personal Studies

Between sessions, you can maximize the impact of the course with the personal studies provided for each week. You can treat each personal study section like a devotional and use them in whatever way works best for your schedule. You could do one section each day for three days of the week or complete them all in one sitting. These personal studies are not intended to be burdensome or time-consuming but to provide a richer experience and continuity between your group sessions.

EVEN PROPHETS GET DEPRESSED

After getting all fired up,
it was almost inevitable that Elijah would cave in.
Depression often comes on the heels of a
spiritual and emotional high.

FROM CHAPTER 1 OF *OUT OF THE CAVE*

Welcome

No matter how strong your faith may be, you likely experience times when frantic thoughts keep you awake at night. Times when your emotions overwhelm you and leave you feeling pulled by their undertow. Moments when you don't know how you will keep going. As you struggle to get through another day, you wonder, "Why do I feel this way?"

You're not alone. Regardless of how long you've followed Jesus, how accomplished you are, or how much money you have, you can still experience times of fear, doubt, anxiety, and depression that rob you of your purpose, peace, and passion. Just like God's prophet Elijah, you may be strong in your faith and suddenly feel like you've fallen into a deep cave of despair. In fact, depression often occurs right after a major spiritual or emotional high point.

Depression is not something you can ignore—and understanding it can help you overcome the stigma often attached to it and other mental illnesses. While many variables are often involved, and biological contributors may require medication as part of treatment, depression also sends a distress signal that your life is out of balance. You must consider all areas of your life as you seek to move forward out of depression.

In this study, we will look at the depression the prophet Elijah faced after he came off the spiritual high point of defeating the prophets of Baal. His story will reveal that we never have to remain in a cave of despair. God is always with us and always willing to lead us out of our personal darkness and into his eternal light.

Share

If you or any of your group members are just getting to know one another, take a few minutes to introduce yourselves. Then, to get things started, discuss one of the following questions:

- What keeps you awake at night? Too much caffeine? Scary movies? Worrying about family? Something else?

— or —

- When you can't sleep at night, what do you do instead? Count sheep? Drink warm milk? Read a book? Get up and eat a snack? Pray? Something else?

Read

Ask one person to read the following passage, and then discuss the questions that follow.

[1] *Now Ahab told Jezebel everything Elijah had done and how he had killed all the prophets with the sword.* [2] *So Jezebel sent a messenger to Elijah to say, "May the gods deal with me, be it ever so severely, if by this time tomorrow I do not make your life like that of one of them."*

[3] *Elijah was afraid and ran for his life. When he came to Beersheba in Judah, he left his servant there,* [4] *while he himself went a day's journey into the wilderness. He came to a broom bush, sat down under it and prayed that he might die. "I have had enough, LORD," he said. "Take my life; I am no better than my ancestors."* [5] *Then he lay down under the bush and fell asleep.*

All at once an angel touched him and said, "Get up and eat." [6] *He looked around, and there by his head was some bread baked over hot coals, and a jar of water. He ate and drank and then lay down again.*

> ⁷ *The angel of the* LORD *came back a second time and touched him and said, "Get up and eat, for the journey is too much for you."* ⁸ *So he got up and ate and drank. Strengthened by that food, he traveled forty days and forty nights until he reached Horeb, the mountain of God.* ⁹ *There he went into a cave and spent the night* (1 Kings 19:1–9).

What do you identify with most in this description of Elijah's descent into depression?

What word, phrase, or image stands out or resonates for you in this passage? Why do you think it strikes a chord right now?

Watch

Play the video segment for session 1 (see the streaming video access provided on the inside front cover). As you watch, use the following outline to record any thoughts that stand out to you.

God called Elijah to warn Israel of impending doom if they continued to reject him and worship idols. Consequently, Elijah arranged a showdown on Mount Carmel with the prophets of Baal, in which God's fire descended and consumed the water-soaked altar.

Ahab, the king of Israel, and his wicked wife, Jezebel, hated Elijah and vowed revenge. Jezebel sent a messenger to tell Elijah that she would kill him within twenty-four hours. This sent the panicked prophet running away into the wilderness.

There are two key observations we can make based on Elijah's experience:

1. Depression often comes on the heels of a spiritual/emotional high.

2. Depression often comes when our minds take over.

Depression can be defined as a mood disorder characterized by anhedonia, extreme sadness, poor concentration, sleep problems, loss of appetite, and feelings of guilt, helplessness, and hopelessness.

There are biological, physical, and neurological factors that contribute to depression and anxiety. Medication may be required as part of treatment. However, if we only focus on these biological factors, we can miss the whole picture.

Many times, we are just afraid to talk about depression because there is a stigma associated with it. *It's okay not to be okay.* When we battle depression, we must remember that God wants to reveal himself in a very special way and make us whole again (see Psalm 46:10, Psalm 16:11, and Isaiah 61:3).

Discuss

Take a few minutes with your group members to discuss what you just heard and explore these concepts in Scripture.

1. Are you surprised that Elijah experienced depression on the heels of such a major spiritual victory? Why or why not?

2. Why do you think Jezebel's threat on his life triggered Elijah's flight impulse? How did her threat get in his head and contribute to his downward spiral?

3. When have circumstances caused you to encounter thoughts and feelings similar to those of Elijah? If you have battled depression and/or anxiety, were there specific events that led up to that struggle?

4. How would you define depression? Explain your answer.

5. Do you agree that experiencing depression may be a distress signal indicating your life is out of balance? Why or why not?

6. What are some of the ways depression and mental illness continue to be stigmatized even by people who follow Jesus? How can we overcome these stigmas in order to help more people experience healing, wholeness, and freedom?

Respond

Briefly review the video teaching outline and any notes you took. Also reflect for a moment on the group discussion you just had. In the space below, write down the most significant point you are taking away from this session—including the teaching, activities, and discussions.

Pray

Go around the room and share any prayer requests you have. Pray for those requests together silently, out loud, or both. Thank God for bringing you all together to study the life of Elijah and to learn more about depression and how to move through it. Ask God to give you wisdom, compassion, and strength as you consider painful chapters in your life and reflect on tough times. Trust that the Lord will protect each of you and guide you in his truth.

PERSONAL STUDY

If you haven't already started reading *Out of the Cave* by Chris Hodges, now is a great time to begin. This week, read the introduction and chapters 1–3 before doing this personal study. The questions and exercises provided in this section are designed to help you receive the greatest benefit from reading the book and applying it to your own life. There will be time for you to share your reflections at the beginning of the next session.

Out of Your Cave

Depression can be a uniquely personal experience that's difficult to describe or express to other people. While Elijah's situation reflects his unique experience, it also reflects a journey through depression that many find similar to their own. Remember how after Elijah's astounding victory, he seemed to plummet rather quickly. He went from the awesome display of God's power and glory on Mount Carmel, which included an embarrassing defeat for King Ahab and the 850 prophets of Baal, to being at the lowest point imaginable—wishing he were dead. Consider the contrast between these high and low points as you read the following passages.

36 At the time of sacrifice, the prophet Elijah stepped forward and prayed: "LORD, the God of Abraham, Isaac and Israel, let it be known today that you are God in Israel and that I am your servant and have done all these things at your command. 37 Answer me, LORD, answer me, so these people will know that you, LORD, are God, and that you are turning their hearts back again."

38 Then the fire of the LORD fell and burned up the sacrifice, the wood, the stones and the soil, and also licked up the water in the trench (1 Kings 18:36–38).

3 Elijah was afraid and ran for his life. When he came to Beersheba in Judah, he left his servant there, 4 while he himself went a day's journey into the wilderness. He came to a broom bush, sat down under it and prayed that he might die. "I have had enough, LORD," he said. "Take my life; I am no better than my ancestors" (1 Kings 19:3–4).

What stands out or strikes you most about these extreme scenes in Elijah's life? Can you relate? When have you gone from a high point to a personal low back-to-back? Looking back, how would you describe your descent?

Do you think the pressure of such a public moment on Mount Carmel contributed to the personal moment Elijah experienced under the broom tree? Why or why not? How do you usually handle the stress and tension between your public life and your private life?

Even after God answered Elijah's prayer in dramatic fashion, a short while later the prophet feared for his life and ran away. When have you doubted God's faithfulness even after you've experienced his power in answer to prayer?

Elijah reached a point where he told God, "I have had enough, Lord." When have you reached a similar breaking point where you cried out, "Enough is enough, Lord! I can't keep going any longer"? How did God answer your prayer then?

What do you think Elijah meant when he told God, "Take my life; I am no better than my ancestors"? What's the connection between Elijah's feelings that he is no better than his ancestors and his desire for his life to end?

Have you ever felt so scared, alone, and defeated that you tried to run away from your problems, either literally or figuratively? What are some ways you sometimes pursue unhealthy escapes when you're feeling low?

Into the Light

You can't begin to come out of your cave until you admit you are in the cave. You have to come clean, acknowledge the problem, and move past any sense of shame or stigma that you have attached to your depression. You can be helped in this regard by recognizing that you aren't the first person to face depression . . . and you won't be the last. In fact, the Bible contains many examples of people who battled such thoughts and feelings. Many of the Psalms, in particular, express feelings of pain, fear, anxiety, and doubt. Often, the psalmist can give voice to what you are struggling to admit. Just consider the following psalm written by King David:

> ¹ *Listen to my prayer, O God,*
> *do not ignore my plea;*
> ² *hear me and answer me.*
> *My thoughts trouble me and I am distraught*
> ³ *because of what my enemy is saying,*
> *because of the threats of the wicked;*
> *for they bring down suffering on me*
> *and assail me in their anger.*
>
> ⁴ *My heart is in anguish within me;*
> *the terrors of death have fallen on me.*
> ⁵ *Fear and trembling have beset me;*
> *horror has overwhelmed me.*
> ⁶ *I said, "Oh, that I had the wings of a dove!*
> *I would fly away and be at rest.*
> ⁷ *I would flee far away*
> *and stay in the desert;*
> ⁸ *I would hurry to my place of shelter,*
> *far from the tempest and storm."*
>
> ¹⁶ *As for me, I call to God,*
> *and the LORD saves me.*
> ¹⁷ *Evening, morning and noon*
> *I cry out in distress,*
> *and he hears my voice* (Psalm 55:1–8, 16–17).

What do you find surprising in the psalmist's disclosures in this passage? Why?

Which of the psalmist's phrases, statements, and questions resonate with you the most? When have you felt this way? What were the circumstances?

When has your "heart been in anguish within you"? How many serious bouts of depression have you experienced in your life?

How have you experienced the stigma attached to depression? What harmful messages and destructive labels were assigned to you or to others around you who have experienced depression?

How has your understanding of depression impacted your relationship with God? When you're feeling low or anxious, have you tended to run toward God or away from him?

What indications of hope does the psalmist express in this passage? What truths give you hope when you're battling similar thoughts and feelings?

Personal Reflection

One of the ways to describe and define depression is to compare it to something else. While Elijah literally ran away and hid in a cave, his journey into interior darkness reflects what depression feels like for many people. Others describe it as being in a fog, or experiencing a slow-moving storm front, or being frozen in place. For this exercise, think about your own experiences with depression and what you've observed in others or learned from reliable sources. Then answer the following questions as you creatively describe and define it.

Depression reminds me of:

The images I associate with depression include:

How would you illustrate your own understanding of depression? What image, metaphor, or picture comes to mind that expresses what you thought and felt during that time? Grab your favorite creative tools—pencil and paper, crayons, markers, paint, whatever you want—and come up with a visual representation of depression that does not rely on words. You can sketch, doodle, draw stick figures, use geometric shapes, paint, color or whatever you enjoy. Don't worry about artistic quality—just find a way to express depression visually.

In preparation for next week, read chapters 4-9 in *Out of the Cave*. Make a note of any key points or questions that you want to share at your next group meeting.

SESSION 2

HOW DID I GET IN THE CAVE?

When we succumb to envy,
we see only the best in others' lives
and the worst in our own.
Envy thrives on comparison.

FROM CHAPTER 5 OF *OUT OF THE CAVE*

Welcome

The first step toward coming out of your cave is to recognize what sent you running there in the first place. In Elijah's story, the queen's threat to kill him caused him to reach his breaking point. "He came to a broom bush, sat down under it and prayed that he might die. 'I have had enough, LORD,' he said. 'Take my life; I am no better than my ancestors'" (1 Kings 19:4).

Notice that once Elijah was in the cave, he began to compare himself to his *ancestors*. The Israelites were known for being fickle and disobedient in their relationship with the Lord. They had grumbled and complained when God led them out of Egypt. They had failed to trust in his word that they could take the Promised Land. When they did conquer it, they had quickly fallen into idolatry and begun worshiping the gods of the Canaanites.

Elijah began to compare himself to *these* ancestors, criticizing himself for being no better. This "comparison trap" drove him deeper into the cave of depression. As we will see in this session, the same will be true of us when we begin to worry too much about what others are thinking and we measure our self-worth against everyone around us.

Share

Take some time to share at least one key takeaway or insight you had from this week's personal studies. Then, to get things started, discuss one of the following questions:

- Have you ever been inside an underground cavern? What was it like?

— *or* —

- Have you ever hiked to a summit? How would you describe your experience?

Read

Ask one person to read the following passage, and then discuss the questions that follow.

> [7] *The angel of the* LORD *came back a second time and touched him and said, "Get up and eat, for the journey is too much for you."* [8] *So he got up and ate and drank. Strengthened by that food, he traveled forty days and forty nights until he reached Horeb, the mountain of God.* [9] *There he went into a cave and spent the night* (1 Kings 19:7–9).

How could Elijah's physical conditional potentially have contributed to his depression?

Why do you think Elijah chose to spend the night in a cave after reaching Mount Horeb?

Watch

Play the video segment for session 2 (see the streaming video access provided on the inside front cover). As you watch, use the following outline to record any thoughts that stand out to you.

Numerous factors contributed to Elijah's descent into the cave of depression (see 1 Kings 19:1–4), the first of which was his life imbalance. Elijah went straight from the victory on Mount Carmel to a lonely place without support.

Second, Elijah was too concerned about what others thought, especially his enemies and critics. When we worry about what others think and compare ourselves to them, we get stuck in our heads, ruminating on thoughts that send us into our cave.

Third, Elijah engaged in negative self-talk. He ruminated and brought up the past. Such thoughts can reinforce our feelings of insecurity and paralyze us emotionally.

Fourth, Elijah left his servant behind and went solo. Depression often leaves us feeling isolated and can cause us to pull away from supportive relationships.

There are several other factors that can contribute to depression:

1. Living without purpose

2. An unbalanced life

3. The burden of guilt

4. An unsupported lifestyle

5. Disconnection from God

We all have a God-sized hole in our heart . . . that only God can fill.

Discuss

Take a few minutes with your group members to discuss what you just heard and explore these concepts in Scripture.

1. How did the choices that Elijah made following his victory on Mount Carmel contribute to his depression? How did his choices reinforce the imbalance in his life?

2. Why did Elijah believe that he was no better than his ancestors? How did this comparison to past generations set him up for depression?

3. How does focusing on what others think make us feel worse about ourselves?

4. Why do you think Elijah left his servant behind and went into the wilderness alone?

5. Which of the issues contributing to depression have you experienced? How did they compound what you were thinking and feeling and make you more depressed?

6. Why is it so important to have supportive relationships when you're battling depression? What are some ways others can help you when you're depressed?

Respond

Briefly review the video teaching outline and any notes you took. Also reflect for a moment on the group discussion you just had. In the space below, write down the most significant point you are taking away from this session—including the teaching, activities, and discussions.

Pray

Wrap up your group time by praying together, lifting up any personal requests or ongoing needs. Thank God for the ways that he sustains you when you're in need of rest and nourishment. Ask him to help you identify any ways that you have fallen into the "comparison trap." Seek his guidance and protection as you consider the factors that can contribute to depression in your life and the lives of those you love.

PERSONAL STUDY

Similar to what you did after session 1, the following questions and exercises will help you apply this week's teaching and practice the personal application. Before you begin, make sure you have finished reading chapters 4–9 in *Out of the Cave*. As you consider this topic, reflect on your responses and ask God to guide you toward the next steps. There will be time for you to share your observations at the beginning of the next session.

Out of Your Cave

As you saw with Elijah, comparison often leads to thoughts and feelings that serve as tinder for depression. When you look at others, it's tempting to assume they have a better, easier, or more enjoyable life. But focusing on your perception of their successes will only lead to insecurity and feelings of personal failure. Take a few minutes to consider how, when, and where comparison, envy, and self-criticism have been present in your life. Use the following questions to help you separate these negative perceptions and false beliefs from the truth of God's Word.

How aware are you of comparing yourself to other people? On a scale of 1 to 10, with 1 being "never or rarely happens" and 10 being "constantly or most of the time," how often do you compare your life to other people's? Explain.

What aspects of your life do you often find coming up short as compared to other people? Check all that apply:

____ Your appearance and physical features
____ Your career and current job
____ Your education level
____ Your athletic ability
____ Your home and where it is located
____ Your vehicle that you drive
____ Your vacations and weekend getaways
____ Your phone, computer, and tech gadgets
____ Your family and their accomplishments
____ Other:

Who is someone you admire and often envy? What is it about his or her life that you wish you had in yours?

How often do you scroll through social media and feel inferior to the friends and family you see posting online? What kinds of posts make you feel this way most often?

How do you usually handle the feelings of jealousy, envy, or dissatisfaction that you experience as a result of comparing yourself to others?

How can such comparisons cause you to lose sight of the way that God made you?

Into the Light

Many of us say that God comes first in our lives, but our time, money, energy, and affections point to other things. We get caught up in acquiring possessions in order to measure up against those with whom we are comparing ourselves. However, this path only leads to dissatisfaction and unfulfillment. Jesus once told the story of a successful man who focused on wealth instead of God. He tore down his barns to build bigger ones so he could store the overflowing abundance of his possessions. This man's life was out of balance, but he didn't realize it until it was too late—a point that Jesus makes clear at the end of the parable.

> [13] *Someone in the crowd said to him, "Teacher, tell my brother to divide the inheritance with me."*
>
> [14] *Jesus replied, "Man, who appointed me a judge or an arbiter between you?"* [15] *Then he said to them, "Watch out! Be on your guard against all kinds of greed; life does not consist in an abundance of possessions."*

¹⁶ *And he told them this parable: "The ground of a certain rich man yielded an abundant harvest.* ¹⁷ *He thought to himself, 'What shall I do? I have no place to store my crops.'*

¹⁸ *"Then he said, 'This is what I'll do. I will tear down my barns and build bigger ones, and there I will store my surplus grain.* ¹⁹ *And I'll say to myself, "You have plenty of grain laid up for many years. Take life easy; eat, drink and be merry."'*

²⁰ *"But God said to him, 'You fool! This very night your life will be demanded from you. Then who will get what you have prepared for yourself?'*

²¹ *"This is how it will be with whoever stores up things for themselves but is not rich toward God."* . . .

³² *"Do not be afraid, little flock, for your Father has been pleased to give you the kingdom.* ³³ *Sell your possessions and give to the poor. Provide purses for yourselves that will not wear out, a treasure in heaven that will never fail, where no thief comes near and no moth destroys.* ³⁴ *For where your treasure is, there your heart will be also* (Luke 12:13–21, 32–34).

Why do you think the man asked Jesus to intervene with his brother in dividing their inheritance? What outcome was this man likely hoping to receive?

How does being blessed with abundant crops lead the man in Jesus's parable into trouble? What does he do as a result?

What does Jesus say about the man's desire to find security in possessions?

What does it mean to be "rich toward God"? How can this kind of spiritual wealth shift your perspective and reduce your tendency to compare yourself to others?

When you consider all areas of your life, how balanced is it right now?

Which areas are out of balance or need attention?

Personal Reflection

Taking a personal inventory of how you spend your time can reveal where your life might be out of balance. Below are twelve areas for you to assess, but feel free to come up with others or make substitutions for what is relevant to your life right now. For each item, rate yourself on a scale of 1–10 to indicate how well you've been maintaining health and balance in that area.

____ Faith
____ Social
____ Marriage

___ Attitude
___ Family
___ Finances
___ Work
___ Creativity
___ Computer
___ Physical
___ Ministry
___ Travel

As you consider all of these areas, what patterns do you see? What stands out to you?

Which areas and activities are affecting your emotions positively?

Which ones are affecting you in a negative way?

How can you redirect those activities that are costing too much energy, time, and focus?

In preparation for next week, read chapters 10–12 in *Out of the Cave*. Make a note of any key points or questions that you want to share at your next group meeting.

REBUILDING OUR EMOTIONAL HOUSE

Elijah's experience reveals that if you want to win
against depression, then you have to let God fill you again.
And that means taking care of the vessel that he has given to you.

FROM CHAPTER 10 OF *OUT OF THE CAVE*

Welcome

We have to be good stewards of the gifts that God has given to us if we want to maintain health and balance in our lives. Neglecting our physical and mental health can make us vulnerable to depression. We see this in the life of Elijah. He ran from his problems, allowed fear to dictate his decisions, and then overlooked basic needs that his body required.

Elijah soon sank into depression beneath the broom bush. He needed sleep and nourishment before he could continue on his journey. So the Lord sent his angel to help Elijah meet these needs before he asked the prophet to deal with other more complex issues. God often reminds us that *we need the same thing.* Before we can continue on our path of healing and restoration, we often just need to be strengthened by sleep and food. Once those needs have been met, we are ready to resume our journey to God's next divine destination.

God invites us to rebuild our "emotional house" today by laying a foundation that is built on our relationship with him and our connectedness to other people. He encourages us to build solid walls of purpose girded by healthy habits and routines to give our lives shape and definition. Such a structure will enable us to confidently navigate adversity, failure, criticism, and change.

Share

Take some time to share at least one key takeaway or insight you had from this week's personal studies. Then, to get things started, discuss one of the following questions:

- What are some of the benefits your present home has provided to you?

— *or* —

- How has your home provided you with a sense of security and protection?

Read

Ask one person to read the following passage, and then discuss the questions that follow.

[24] *"Therefore everyone who hears these words of mine and puts them into practice is like a wise man who built his house on the rock.* [25] *The rain came down, the streams rose, and the winds blew and beat against that house; yet it did not fall, because it had its foundation on the rock.* [26] *But everyone who hears these words of mine and does not put them into practice is like a foolish man who built his house on sand.* [27] *The rain came down, the streams rose, and the winds blew and beat against that house, and it fell with a great crash"* (Matthew 7:24–27).

Why do you think Jesus chose the metaphor of building a house to contrast the difference between those who practice his teachings and those who do not?

What is one way that you have learned to build your house on rock instead of sand? How has this kept the foundation of your life secure?

Watch

Play the video segment for session 3 (see the streaming video access provided on the inside front cover). As you watch, use the following outline to record any thoughts that stand out to you.

Crisis inevitably reveals our emotional capacity and strength of character. When faith in Christ is our bedrock foundation, we are ready when life's storms hit.

The first thing God did for Elijah was to address his needs for food, water, and sleep. Once Elijah's body was restored, he was ready to take the next step on his journey.

The *soul* can be defined as your mind, your will, and your emotions.

Jesus used the metaphor of a house built on rock to describe how your soul is able to withstand the storms of life. You can build your *emotional* house to handle adversity.

Your soul, just like a physical house, is made up of three areas:

1. Foundation: relationships and connectedness

2. Frame: purpose and routines

3. Finishes: trust and self-control

The great psychologist Dr. George W. Crane wrote, "Motions are the precursors of emotions." If you take the right steps, it can actually affect how you feel.

Discuss

Take a few minutes with your group members to discuss what you just heard and explore these concepts in Scripture.

1. What stands out as you consider the way in which God first met Elijah's physical needs before anything else? Have you ever experienced a situation that required you to prioritize addressing your physical needs?

2. Why are relationships with God and other people essential to the strength of your house's foundation? What happens when you try to be self-sufficient and independent?

3. How does living out your life's purpose provide structure for your house? What are ways your habits and routines are presently helping to support the purpose you're living out?

4. When have you changed your daily habits and routines to restore balance in your life? What happened as a result?

5. What do you need to change or adjust based on your needs right now? How will you seek to do this?

6. How have you learned to trust God for those things that you can't control? How do you tell the difference between what *you* need to do and what you need to allow *God* to do?

Respond

Briefly review the video teaching outline and any notes you took. Also reflect for a moment on the group discussion you just had. In the space below, write down the most significant point you are taking away from this session—including the teaching, activities, and discussions.

Pray

Wrap up your group time by praying together, lifting up any personal requests or ongoing needs. Thank God for the ways that he has provided just what you needed in the past, and express your willingness to trust him to continue providing what you need in the future. Ask him to strengthen your emotional house and give you wisdom about the parts that need reinforcement. Praise him for who he is and how much he loves you.

PERSONAL STUDY

Now that you're becoming more aware of the factors that can set you up for depression, it's time to begin making changes in areas you can control. Consider the ways you take care of your basic needs and think about what resonates with you the most as you look at Elijah's story. Before you begin, make sure you have read chapters 10–12 in *Out of the Cave*. Again, there will be time for you to share your observations at the beginning of the next session.

Out of Your Cave

We all have been blindsided by circumstances that roll into our lives like a fast-moving thunderstorm and leave us feeling vulnerable and depleted. If we want to protect ourselves from such storms, we have to strengthen the "components" of our emotional house and take care of our basic physical needs. In Elijah's story, it is clear that he was evidently neglecting some of those basic needs for his body, mind, and soul. This lack of basic self-care is highlighted by the way that God sends an angel to help Elijah get back on his feet . . . literally. Read the following passage once more and circle any words or phrases that stand out to you:

⁵ Then he lay down under the bush and fell asleep. All at once an angel touched him and said, "Get up and eat." ⁶ He looked around, and there by his head was some bread baked over hot coals, and a jar of water. He ate and drank and then lay down again. ⁷ The angel of the LORD came back a second time and touched him and said, "Get up and eat, for the journey is too much for you." ⁸ So he got up and ate and drank. Strengthened by that food, he traveled forty days and forty nights until he reached Horeb, the mountain of God (1 Kings 19:5–8).

Look back at what you circled in the passage above. What word, phrase, or image stands out the most to you? Why do you think that jumped out at you?

When has God forced you to rest, change your diet, or take some other step for your physical health? Did you see the benefits of these changes or resist making them?

How often do you check in with yourself to ensure that you are getting enough rest and sleep? How have you sabotaged your attempts to rest?

How well does your current diet provide fuel and nutrition for your body? What is one small change you could make today to be kinder to your body?

When was the last time you unplugged and spent a few hours just resting and relaxing? Why is it often so hard to turn off the distractions and just enjoy peace and quiet?

What is one habit related to your body's basic needs that you could change or improve? How can you spend more time truly resting your body, mind, and soul?

Into the Light

God always knows what is best for us. He wants to provide the rest and peace that we need to maintain both our physical and spiritual health. Each day, he calls us to heed his voice as he leads us through "dark valleys" and into "green pastures." David's words in Psalm 23 illustrate this beautifully. While the psalm may be familiar, read through it and assess where you are in your relationship with God and what you need from him. Use the questions that follow to help you consider what is required on your part to experience the kind of refreshment and renewal that is described in the psalm.

¹ *The* LORD *is my shepherd, I lack nothing.*
  ² *He makes me lie down in green pastures,*
he leads me beside quiet waters,
   ³ *he refreshes my soul.*
He guides me along the right paths
   for his name's sake.
⁴ *Even though I walk*
   through the darkest valley,
I will fear no evil,
   for you are with me;
your rod and your staff,
   they comfort me.

⁵ *You prepare a table before me*
   in the presence of my enemies.
You anoint my head with oil;
   my cup overflows.
⁶ *Surely your goodness and love will follow me*
   all the days of my life,
and I will dwell in the house of the LORD
   forever.

On average, how often in a given week do you spend time lingering in "green pastures" or resting "beside quiet waters" for spiritual refreshment?

What practical steps can you take to enjoy more time alone with your Good Shepherd?

When have you recently experienced the kind of soul rest and spiritual refreshment the psalmist describes ? What impact did this have on other areas of your life?

What image or description stands out the most to you in this psalm? Why do you think that image or description resonates so much in your life right now?

What does it look like for God to prepare a table before you in the presence of your enemies? How can you experience his rest and peace despite stressful circumstances?

Jesus said that he is the Good Shepherd and that his sheep follow him because they know his voice (see John 10:4). How well do you know your Good Shepherd's voice? Where do you sense that he is leading you currently in your life?

Personal Reflection

If you wish to receive the same help that God gave to Elijah, you must be willing to assess your lifestyle and the toll it is taking on you physically and mentally. You may already know some changes that need to be made in order to practice better self-care. But if you're serious about overcoming depression, it is time to face the truth and actually *make* those needed changes. Use the following questions to begin this process, asking the Holy Spirit to guide you.

- **Diet:** Are your eating habits contributing to or taking away from your health? What is one thing you can cut back on right away?

- **Sleep:** Are you getting enough sleep every night (seven or more hours)? How can you eliminate those things that are preventing you from sleeping well?

- **Social:** Are you connecting in life-giving relationships with others? What can you do to better nurture these relationships?

- **Hobbies:** Do you engage in activities that rejuvenate your mind and heart? When was the last time you enjoyed pursuing these hobbies?

- **Exercise:** Do you have a consistent routine to keep your body healthy? What can you start to do to begin exercising more regularly?

- **Down Time:** Do you make time for reflection and solitude? How can you fill your time with things that nourish and replenish you?

Review your responses and what you see from the big picture. Choose one area of improvement and one action step that you will take today. Write it below:

Area of improvement that I will address:

One action step that I will take:

In preparation for next week, read chapter 13 in *Out of the Cave*. Make a note of any key points or questions that you want to share at your next group meeting.

DREAM AGAIN

Dreams pull you out of the black-and-white shadows of the cave
by adding color, light, and texture to your life's purpose.

FROM CHAPTER 13 OF *OUT OF THE CAVE*

Welcome

Elijah had lost his ability to see things clearly. He needed God's perspective. After the Lord tended to his physical needs, he gave that perspective to him. Even though Elijah had retreated to a cave, God met him there and demonstrated in a powerful way that he was still in control, still all-powerful, and still the same God whom Elijah had been serving all along.

But the Lord also revealed himself to Elijah in a more subtle way. After revealing his power to the prophet through a mighty wind, an earthquake, and a fire, the Lord called out to Elijah *through a gentle whisper.* In our own lives, while we may want God to reveal his presence in a spectacular way every time, we find that he often prefers to simply whisper to us . . . gently reminding us that he is present with us and involved in the situation we are facing.

Although overcoming depression is a process, there is no substitute for a single moment of experiencing the power and presence of God. Knowing him personally and intimately is the greatest antidepressant available in our spiritual battle for health and wholeness. Rarely do we experience instant curative healing from our depression, but a fresh awareness of God's presence and perspective in our lives can quickly get us moving and dreaming again.

Share

Take some time to share at least one key takeaway or insight you had from this week's personal studies. Then, to get things started, discuss one of the following questions:

- When has God spoken to you through a spectacular event or set of circumstances? How did you respond?

  — *or* —

- When has God spoken to you through a quiet and gentle whisper? How did you respond?

Read

Ask one person to read the following passage, and then discuss the questions that follow.

⁹*And the word of the LORD came to him: "What are you doing here, Elijah?"*

¹⁰ *He replied, "I have been very zealous for the LORD God Almighty. The Israelites have rejected your covenant, torn down your altars, and put your prophets to death with the sword. I am the only one left, and now they are trying to kill me too."*

¹¹ *The LORD said, "Go out and stand on the mountain in the presence of the LORD, for the LORD is about to pass by."*

Then a great and powerful wind tore the mountains apart and shattered the rocks before the LORD, but the LORD was not in the wind. After the wind there was an earthquake, but the LORD was not in the earthquake. ¹² *After the earthquake came a fire, but the LORD was not in the fire. And after the fire came a gentle whisper.* ¹³ *When Elijah heard it, he pulled his cloak over his face and went out and stood at the mouth of the cave.*

Then a voice said to him, "What are you doing here, Elijah?"

¹⁴ *He replied, "I have been very zealous for the LORD God Almighty. The Israelites have rejected your covenant, torn down your altars, and put your prophets to death with the sword. I am the only one left, and now they are trying to kill me too."*

> [15] *The LORD said to him, "Go back the way you came, and go to the Desert of Damascus. When you get there, anoint Hazael king over Aram.* [16] *Also, anoint Jehu son of Nimshi king over Israel, and anoint Elisha son of Shaphat from Abel Meholah to succeed you as prophet.* [17] *Jehu will put to death any who escape the sword of Hazael, and Elisha will put to death any who escape the sword of Jehu.* [18] *Yet I reserve seven thousand in Israel—all whose knees have not bowed down to Baal and whose mouths have not kissed him"* (1 Kings 19:9–18).

Why do you think that God asked Elijah what he was doing there? After all, wasn't God the one who invited him to Mount Horeb?

What word, phrase, or image jumps out in this conversation that Elijah has with God? Why do you think it resonates with you?

Watch

Play the video segment for session 4 (see the streaming video access provided on the inside front cover). As you watch, use the following outline to record any thoughts that stand out to you.

We tend to look at failure and think we are disqualified from ever influencing others again. But that's not how God sees it.

He wants us to get healthy and be restored to him so we can get back in the game. God wants us to dream again.

God reminded Elijah about his calling and told him to "go back the way you came." He wanted Elijah to go back to that place where he committed to serve the Lord.

If we don't have a clear vision for our lives, we will think that it doesn't matter how we live. When we are idle—when we don't have *purpose*—we make bad choices.

The quickest way to defeat depression is to start serving the needs of other people. You must dare to dream again and do something that calls you to act.

There are five things you can do that will help you get a dream from God:

1. Get alone with God.

2. Make a fresh commitment to God's Word.

3. Write down a God-sized dream.

4. Wake up and do something.

5. Don't give up on your dream.

It takes great endurance to see your dream fulfilled. Getting a dream is the easy part . . . but believing God for it and persevering is what is so important.

Discuss

Take a few minutes with your group members to discuss what you just heard and explore these concepts in Scripture.

1. Review 1 Kings 19:10. What emotions did Elijah express in his response to God's question? How did Elijah justify feeling the way that he felt?

2. Why do you think God repeated his initial question—"What are you doing here, Elijah?" (verse 13)—after the prophet responded the way he did? What did Elijah communicate to God when he gave the *exact same response* again?

3. Why do you think God's whisper caught Elijah's attention more than the great wind, the earthquake, or the fire?

4. What evidence do you see in Elijah's response that he had lost his purpose as God's prophet? How did his sense of loneliness reinforce what he felt he had lost?

5. When have you similarly felt as if you had lost focus on your life's purpose? What did God reveal to help you find your next step?

6. What dream is God whispering to you right now? What ministry, cause, or need is stirring your passion to serve and advance God's kingdom?

Respond

Briefly review the video teaching outline and any notes you took. Also reflect for a moment on the group discussion you just had. In the space below, write down the most significant point you are taking away from this session—including the teaching, activities, and discussions.

Pray

Before you end your time together with prayer, go around the group and share one personal request related to the dream that God has given you for your life. You don't need to go into detail or explain your dream, but let others know enough so they can lift up your request. Then begin your prayer time by thanking God for the ways he continues to speak to you. Give him thanks and praise for the many ways that he is at work in your life, igniting and empowering dreams that only you can accomplish for his purposes. Ask him to inspire you with a fresh vision and renewed sense of purpose as you continue to leave "the cave" behind you.

PERSONAL STUDY

As you saw in the video teaching this week, having a fresh encounter with God is essential to getting out of your cave and starting the process of dreaming again. Before you begin this week's study, make sure you have read chapter 13 in Out *of the Cave*. Be sure to record your reflections and observations in this study guide so you can share them with your group.

Out of Your Cave

Even when you know that God has a purpose and plan for your life, it can still be overwhelming to come out of your cave and take the steps toward your assignment. This will be especially true when you feel crippled by circumstances or paralyzed by painful emotions. But you *can* move forward, even when you're in distress or in the fog of depression.

It helps to keep in mind that life is not fair—at least, not from our earthly, human perspective. Jesus was clear on this point: "[God] causes his sun to rise on the evil and the good, and sends rain on the righteous and the unrighteous" (Matthew 5:45). But the Lord was equally clear that our lives always have meaning . . .

even in our most painful situations: "'For I know the plans I have for you,' declares the LORD, 'plans to prosper you and not to harm you, plans to give you hope and a future'" (Jeremiah 29:11).

As followers of Christ, we are called to participate in the process of using what we have learned through our own painful experiences to help alleviate the sufferings of others. The apostle Paul put it this way: "God is our merciful Father and the source of all comfort. He comforts us in all our troubles so that we can comfort others. When they are troubled, we will be able to give them the same comfort God has given us" (2 Corinthians 1:3–4 NLT).

How do you usually handle the unfairness you encounter in life? What injustice or unfair situation are you presently facing?

When have you been able to help, encourage, or minister to someone because you have experienced what they are going through? How did serving them make you feel?

Who has supported you during times of struggle because of what they have already overcome? How did their testimony motivate you to keep going and persevere?

Looking back, how have you been able to see glimpses of God at work in spite of the trials that you have faced? (It's okay if you're still waiting on him, so don't feel like there's a "right answer." Remember, it's okay not to be okay!)

When has comforting someone else brought you a deeper sense of God's comfort? Why do you think this happens?

How is God leading you to draw on your past experiences to bless others right now?

Into the Light

When we are wrestling with our thoughts, feelings, doubts, and pains, it can often feel like some invisible force is preventing us from taking a step toward God. We want to get up and go to the mouth of our cave, but we can't. There is just no energy, no hope, no sense of initiative. Perhaps the best-known wrestler in the Bible is Jacob. He seemed to know the painful struggle of wrestling—with himself, with his family, with God—better than anyone. But Jacob's *willingness* to wrestle changed the direction of his life.

> [22] *That night Jacob got up and took his two wives, his two female servants and his eleven sons and crossed the ford of the Jabbok.*

²³ *After he had sent them across the stream, he sent over all his possessions.* ²⁴ *So Jacob was left alone, and a man wrestled with him till daybreak.* ²⁵ *When the man saw that he could not overpower him, he touched the socket of Jacob's hip so that his hip was wrenched as he wrestled with the man.* ²⁶ *Then the man said, "Let me go, for it is daybreak."*

But Jacob replied, "I will not let you go unless you bless me."

²⁷ *The man asked him, "What is your name?"*

"Jacob," he answered.

²⁸ *Then the man said, "Your name will no longer be Jacob, but Israel, because you have struggled with God and with humans and have overcome."*

²⁹ *Jacob said, "Please tell me your name."*

But he replied, "Why do you ask my name?" Then he blessed him there.

So Jacob called the place Peniel, saying, "It is because I saw God face to face, and yet my life was spared" (Genesis 32:22–30).

How is Jacob's experience wrestling in this place similar to Elijah's encounter with God on Mount Horeb? What are the key differences?

Why did Jacob refuse to let go of his wrestling partner until he received a blessing? When have you received a blessing by persevering and refusing to give up?

What limps or scars do you have as a result of past "wrestling matches"? How do they serve as reminders of God's presence in your life?

Elijah and Jacob both wrestled for a new sense of purpose and identity. How have you wrestled through challenges in order to be more of who God created you to be?

What past mistakes continue to cloud your thinking and obscure your vision? How can you wrestle through those mistakes to discover God's next assignment?

When has "wrestling" with God been a necessary part of your spiritual growth? How is your faith stronger because of your willingness to wrestle through hard issues?

Personal Reflection

The apostle Paul had many reasons to be depressed about his life and ministry—persecution, assaults, arrest, jail time, shipwrecks, snake bites . . . you name it. But Paul's purpose in life gave him the strength to suffer, endure, and persevere. He explained how we, as followers of Jesus, can experience that same peace and perspective even when life's storms overwhelm us:

¹⁶ *Therefore we do not lose heart. Though outwardly we are wasting away, yet inwardly we are being renewed day by day.* ¹⁷ *For our light and momentary troubles are achieving for us an eternal glory that far outweighs them all.* ¹⁸ *So we fix our eyes not on what is seen, but on what is unseen, since what is seen is temporary, but what is unseen is eternal* (2 Corinthians 4:16–18).

Paul knew it is important to focus on what is *eternal* rather than *temporary*. As you consider what it means for you to dream again, try to focus on the next step God is asking you to take. Complete the following sentences as a way to jumpstart your momentum.

The God-given dream that I am most passionate about pursuing is:

God has already prepared and equipped me to fulfill this dream through past experiences such as:

He has also blessed me with talents, abilities, and gifts like:

I know this dream will minister to others and serve God's kingdom because:

The next step I need to take in making this dream a reality is:

Toward this end, today I will take this step:

In preparation for next week, read chapter 14 and the appendices in *Out of the Cave*. Make a note of any key points or questions that you want to share at your next group meeting.

WE NEED EACH OTHER

Relationships provide the best insurance against cave-ins.

FROM CHAPTER 14 OF *OUT OF THE CAVE*

Welcome

By now, we know that no one is immune from depression—not even a prophet like Elijah! We've discussed how depression often results from (or is compounded by) unhealthy habits and an imbalanced life. We've seen that by focusing on what we can control—building and maintaining a strong "emotional house"—we can protect ourselves from the brunt of life's storms and unexpected losses. We've also seen that one of the most effective ways to overcome depression is to dream again and to focus on serving others.

In the final session, we arrive at the last strategy that God gave to Elijah to move him out of the cave of depression and into the next stage of his life: *relationships and healthy community.* Once Elijah accepted God's new mission, he left his cave and never again (at least that we know) experienced depression. Instead, he worked to fulfill the assignment that God gave him and poured his life into teaching and mentoring Elisha, his successor.

Through their example, we are reminded that God never intended for us to walk alone through life. We all want to be needed and we all want to be known. We all have experiences and abilities that can bless others in countless ways, which in turn bless us. Christ-centered relationships provide the final and critical ingredient that God offers us to get out of our cave.

Share

Take some time to share at least one key takeaway or insight you had from this week's personal studies. Then, to get things started, discuss one of the following questions:

- Who was your best friend as you were growing up? Are you still in contact?

— or —

• How would you describe the friendships that you currently have in your life?

Read

Ask one person to read the following passage, and then discuss the questions that follow.

[19] *So Elijah went from there and found Elisha son of Shaphat. He was plowing with twelve yoke of oxen, and he himself was driving the twelfth pair. Elijah went up to him and threw his cloak around him.* [20] *Elisha then left his oxen and ran after Elijah. "Let me kiss my father and mother goodbye," he said, "and then I will come with you."*

"Go back," Elijah replied. "What have I done to you?"

[21] *So Elisha left him and went back. He took his yoke of oxen and slaughtered them. He burned the plowing equipment to cook the meat and gave it to the people, and they ate. Then he set out to follow Elijah and became his servant* (1 Kings 19:19–21).

What strikes you about the way in which Elisha committed to Elijah in this passage?

How might you have responded if Elijah had thrown his cloak on *your* shoulders?

Watch

Play the video segment for session 5 (see the streaming video access provided on the inside front cover). As you watch, use the following outline to record any thoughts that stand out to you.

God never intended for us to walk through life alone. We all want to be needed and known. Christ-centered relationships are the final ingredients to get us out of the cave.

Elijah learned the lesson of trying to do life alone. He partnered with a young protégé named Elisha. He threw his cloak on him, which is a sign of covenant relationship.

Our lives are not shaped by information but by relationships. "Just as our bodies have many parts and each part has a special function, so it is with Christ's body. We are many parts of one body, and we all belong to each other" (Romans 12:5 NLT).

The Johari Window is a tool for exploring different aspects of your life and relationships with others. There are four quadrants in the Johari Window:

1. Arena: I know and you know.

2. Mask: I know but you don't know.

3. Blind spots: I don't know but you know.

4. Potential: I don't know and you don't know.

God created us to be relational beings. To come out of our cave, we need each other.

Discuss

Take a few minutes with your group members to discuss what you just heard and explore these concepts in Scripture.

1. What do you imagine Elisha was thinking when Elijah placed his cloak on his shoulders in the field? What do you think Elisha expected from his new mentor?

2. Elijah agrees to allow Elisha to "go back" to his parents and states he has not put any constraints on the younger man. Why do you think Elijah allowed him to do this? What did Elijah understand about the sacrifice he was asking Elisha to make?

3. What sacrifices do you need to make to grow closer to others in Christian community?

4. Who has poured their life into you—even if only for a brief season—in a way that made an ongoing positive difference in your life?

5. What benefits do you see in using a tool like the Johari Window? How can it help you in the way you see yourself and your relationships with others?

6. How have your relationships with believers helped you when you've been down or battling depression? How have you helped others during their time in the cave?

Respond

Briefly review the video teaching outline and any notes you took. Also, reflect for a moment on the group discussion you just had. In the space below, write down the most significant point you are taking away from this session—including the teaching, activities, and discussions.

Pray

As you conclude this last group session, go around the room and share any prayer requests you would like others to pray about, as well as one thing you're grateful to have gained through this group. Thank God for all that he has shown you, taught you, and given you through this small-group study. Ask for his continued blessings on each of you as the group completes this time together.

PERSONAL STUDY

Now that you've completed all five sessions, use these final questions and exercises to help you reflect and evaluate your experience and all that you have learned. Make sure you finish reading *Out of the Cave* before completing this study. As you will see, you will be asked to remain in touch with other group members so you can continue to encourage and uphold one another in prayer. This is a great way to practice last week's lesson on how we need each other.

Out of Your Cave

Begin this final time of personal study by making a gratitude list. Write down some of the things you especially appreciate from your time with the group, from reading the book, and from completing this study. Feel free to make your own list or use these prompts to get you started.

I am thankful for this group because:

I am grateful that I have recently learned:

I thank God for blessing my life with:

Into the Light

Staying out of the cave of depression and helping others move out of their caves requires trust in God and healthy relationships with others. As you restore balance, experience healing, pursue your God-given dreams, and build relationships, rely on the Lord's power to sustain you. Remember that he is your loving Father who created you for his special purposes. He wants you to be fulfilled and for your life to be meaningful. Keep this in mind as you read the following passage and complete the questions that follow.

> [4] *Rejoice in the Lord always. I will say it again: Rejoice!* [5] *Let your gentleness be evident to all. The Lord is near.* [6] *Do not be anxious about anything, but in every situation, by prayer and petition, with thanksgiving, present your requests to God.* [7] *And the peace of God, which transcends all understanding, will guard your hearts and your minds in Christ Jesus.*
>
> [8] *Finally, brothers and sisters, whatever is true, whatever is noble, whatever is right, whatever is pure, whatever is lovely, whatever is admirable—if anything is excellent or praiseworthy—think about such things.* [9] *Whatever you have learned or received or heard from me, or seen in me—put it into practice. And the God of peace will be with you* (Philippians 4:4–9).

What is the remedy for worry and anxiety? How does praying, giving thanks, and presenting your requests to God shift your focus away from depression?

When have you experienced "the peace of God, which transcends all understanding"? How does God's peace empower you to deal with difficult circumstances?

How can making your gentleness evident to others build your community?

On average, how often do you think about the things mentioned in this passage?

What does this passage reveal about the importance of Christian community? How do we help each other grow closer to God?

Do you have the community of Christ-followers necessary to support you through life's storms? How can you show them how much they mean to you?

Personal Reflection

As you discussed in this session, healthy relationships and a Christian community are essential to overcoming depression. With this truth in mind, think back on each of your group members and what they contributed to your experience. Use the following questions to help you bring closure to this study as you continue to pursue Jesus and the life he has for you outside the cave.

What are some of the specific moments, people, and words from your group's meetings for which you're particularly thankful?

What is something that you learned through this group that surprised you? How will knowing this impact you moving forward?

What will you carry with you now that your group has concluded this study? How have you changed since starting and completing these sessions?

Which group member or members had the greatest impact on your experience with this study? How did they bless you with their words, questions, prayers, and actions?

Choose at least one other member from your group and send them a text, email, or call him or her to see how things are going. Ask who the person chose to reach out to from your group, and make sure that everyone in your group hears from someone else. If the group wants to continue meeting, make a plan for your next study. Or, if the group disbands, continue checking on the friends you made and asking how you can pray for them.

Leader's Guide

Thank you for agreeing to lead a small group through this study! What you have chosen to do is valuable and will make a great difference in the lives of others.

Out of the Cave is a five-session Bible study built around video content and small-group interaction. As the group leader, just think of yourself as the host of a dinner party. Your job is to take care of your guests by managing all the behind-the-scenes details so that when everyone arrives, they can just enjoy time together.

As the group leader, your role is not to answer all the questions or re-teach the content—the video, book, and study guide will do most of that work. Your job is to guide the experience and create an environment where people can process, question, and reflect—not receive more instruction.

Make sure everyone gets a copy of the study guide. Also make sure they are aware that they have access to the videos at any time through the streaming code provided on the inside front cover. This will keep everyone on the same page and help the process run more smoothly. If some group members are unable to purchase the guide, see if some of your group members can share the resource. Giving everyone access to all the materials will position this study to be as rewarding as possible. Everyone should feel free to write in their study guides and bring them to group every week.

Setting Up the Group

As the group leader, you'll want to create an environment that encourages sharing and learning. A church sanctuary or classroom may not be as ideal as a living room, because those locations can feel formal and less intimate. No matter what setting you choose, provide enough comfortable seating for everyone, and, if possible, arrange the seats in a semicircle so everyone can see the video easily. This will make transition between the video and group conversation more efficient and natural.

Also, try to get to the meeting site early so you can greet participants as they arrive. Simple refreshments create a welcoming atmosphere and can be a wonderful addition to a group study evening as well. Try to take food and pet allergies into account to make your guests as comfortable as possible. You may also want to consider offering childcare for couples with children who want to attend. Finally, be sure your media technology is working properly. Managing these details up front will make the rest of your group experience flow smoothly and provide a welcoming space in which to engage with the content of *Out of the Cave*.

Starting Your Group Time

Once everyone has arrived, it's time to begin the group. Here are some simple tips to make your group time more healthy, enjoyable, and effective.

First, consider beginning the meeting with a short prayer, and remind the group members to put their phones on silent. This is a way to make sure you can all be present with one another and with God. Then, give each person one or two minutes to respond to the questions in the "Share" section. You won't need much time in session 1, but beginning in session 2, people will likely need more time to share their insights from their personal studies and to enjoy getting better acquainted. Usually, you won't answer the discussion questions yourself, but you may need to go first a couple of times and set an example, answering briefly and with a reasonable amount of transparency.

At the end of session 1, invite the group members to complete the "between-sessions" personal studies for that week. Let them know that if they choose to do so, they can watch the video for the following week by accessing the streaming code found on the inside front cover of their study guides. Explain that you will be providing some time before the video teaching the following week for anyone to share reflections from their personal study time. Let them know sharing is optional, and it's no problem if they can't always get to the between-session activities. It will still be beneficial for them to hear from the other participants and learn about what they discovered.

During the "Share" section, help those group members who completed the personal studies to debrief their experiences. Debriefing something like this is a bit different from responding to questions based on the video, because the content comes from the participants' real lives. The basic experiences that you want the group to reflect on are:

- *What was the best part about this week's personal study?*
- *What was the hardest part?*
- *What did I learn about myself?*
- *What did I learn about God?*

Feel free to expand on this time or adapt the questions based on the dynamics of your group.

Leading the Discussion Time

Now that the group is engaged, it's time to watch the video and respond with some directed small-group discussion. Encourage all the group members to participate in the discussion. As the discussion progresses, you may want to follow up with comments such as, "Tell me more about that," or, "Why did you answer that way?"

This will allow the group participants to deepen their reflections and invite meaningful sharing in a way that makes them feel safe.

Note that you have been given multiple questions to use in each session, and you do not have to use them all or even follow them in order. Feel free to pick and choose questions based on either the needs of your group or how the conversation is flowing. Also, don't be afraid of silence. Offering a question and allowing up to thirty seconds of silence is okay. It allows people space to think about how they want to respond and also gives them time to do so.

As group leader, you are the boundary keeper. Do not let anyone (yourself included) dominate the group time. Keep an eye out for group members who might be tempted to "attack" folks they disagree with or try to "fix" those having struggles. These kinds of behaviors can derail a group's momentum, so they need to be steered in a different direction. Model active listening and encourage everyone in your group to do the same. This will make your group time a safe space and create a positive community.

The group discussion time leads to a closing individual activity (the "Respond" section). During this time, encourage the participants to take just a few minutes to review what they've learned and write down a key takeaway. This will help them cement the big ideas in their minds as you close the session. End your time together with prayer as a group.

Thank you again for taking the time to lead your group. You are making a difference in the lives of others and having an impact for the kingdom of God.

If You Enjoyed the 5-Session Video Study, Make Sure You Don't Miss Reading the Book.

Depression is the #1 health issue in our world, yet those who suffer are still stigmatized. *Out of the Cave* shows how to step into the light when depression darkens what you see.

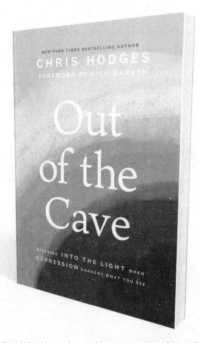

With a blend of Bible-based wisdom, practical application, and personal vulnerability, Chris Hodges explores the causes of depression we can't change, the contributors we can conquer, and offers transformative hope to help us win the battle.

OutOfTheCave.com

AVAILABLE WHEREVER BOOKS ARE SOLD.

Do you find yourself asking, "What do I do next? How do I stay motivated to grow deeper in my relationship with God when I feel complacent, intimidated, or confused? What can I do to get back on track when I hit a spiritual rut?" In *What's Next?*, bestselling author and pastor Chris Hodges offers a practical guide to all those looking for clarity and direction, and reveals the four steps to spiritual maturity.

In this five-session video Bible study and book Chris demonstrates how each step is part of both a linear path and a cycle leading to deeper levels of faith. No matter where you may be on the spiritual spectrum, *What's Next?* is the guide you need to find your next step, and discover the joy that comes walking the road of richer faith.

Book	Study Guide	DVD
9780718091569	9780310104124	9780310104148

Available now at your favorite bookstore,
or streaming video on StudyGateway.com.